MW01196695

Spiritual Money
SEVEN TRUTHS THAT WILL SET YOU FREE

Michelle LaBrosse, PMP

**MAKLAF
PRESS**

Carson City, Nevada

Spiritual Money®: Seven Truths That Will Set You Free

by Michelle LaBrosse, PMP

Published by Maklaf Press LLC.

502 N. Division St., Carson City, NV 89703

A Division of MAKLAF Holding Inc.

www.cheetahlearning.com

Notice: This publication contains the opinions and ideas of the author. It is intended to provide helpful and informative material on the subject matter covered. It is not meant to replace the advice of an attorney. The author and publisher specifically disclaim any responsibility for any liability, loss, or risk, personal or otherwise, that is incurred as a consequence, directly or indirectly, of the use and/or application of any of the contents of this book.

Reference to a product, service, or company does not imply recommendation, approval, affiliation, or sponsorship of that product, service, or company by either the authors or MAKLAF Press.

MAKLAF Press books are available at special quantity discounts to use as premiums and sales promotions, or for use in corporate training programs. For more information, please write to the Director of Sales, MAKALF Press, 502 N. Division Street, Carson City, Nevada 89703, or contact your local bookstore. Visit www.maklafpress.com.

Publisher's Cataloging-in-Publication Data

(Prepared by The Donohue Group, Inc.)

Spiritual Money®:/LaBrosse, Michelle

ISBN:

0-9761749-4-4—10 digit format

978-0-9761749-4-3—13 digit format

1. Finances 2. Goal Attainment 3. Making Money

First Printing 2008

To a peaceful, positive and prosperous future for all.

Michelle LaBrosse, PMP

Preface

"Count on relationships, not on credit to solve your problems," says successful business owner Michelle LaBrosse in this simple, seven-point guide to prosperity. Despite the current economic turmoil, entrepreneurs, consumers and anyone in a financial crunch in the wake of the Wall Street Meltdown now have a practical guide to improving their finances.

"All you need to do is rethink your relationship to money," says LaBrosse. "Survival is all about attitude. If you're more interested in creating value for others than in what you can get from the situation, you'll have all the money you'll ever need."

According to its energetic author, *Spiritual Money*® (www.spiritualmoney.com) is a call to arms for a new paradigm in personal finance and fulfillment. As one of the world's most influential women in Project Management, Michelle knows what she is talking about as she has lost all of her money, not once, but twice.

LaBrosse is no stranger to challenge. In fact, she admits that personal hardship is often the greatest motivator. By 1996 she was divorced, had two failed businesses behind her, and had to figure out how to support her children on her own. She took a job that provided needed income, but it did not feed her soul. After three years at the feed trough of corporate America, she gave up an unfulfilling high-paying job to share the best of her talents with the world through her business called Cheetah Learning. (www.cheetahlearning.com). Living on a wing and a prayer, Michelle gave up the car she had on payments and downsized her life overall. No bank would loan her money for her business, so she used the concepts now shared in Spiritual Money to make it all happen.

By applying the principles of her specialty, Project Management, she built her business in less than four years from zero to nearly $10 million in sales, earning a chapter in the book "Rich Dad, Poor Dad Success Stories." Her Spiritual Money techniques enabled her to do this without using credit cards or bank loans. And she did this as a single mom while her children were still in elementary school (in other words, still very young and dependent). To this day, Michelle still refuses to own a credit card.

Michelle first wrote Spiritual Money in 2003 as a historical record so her family would be able to reproduce her success. At the time, others weren't interested in her concepts because of a false sense of prosperity driven by easy credit. With the current financial crises, Michelle heard a call to action. She is now making the concepts that have driven her own success available to everyone.

"We're at war with money," says LaBrosse. "My book teaches you how to make peace with money to achieve ultimate success."

To this end, her succinct, practical guide covers:

- How to develop an action plan to radically change your relationship to money and success.

- Techniques for incorporating change quickly and easily into day-to-day economic and personal choices.

- Why it's more important to invest in satisfying personal relationships based on service.

"Most people don't make the connection between their feelings about money and success," adds LaBrosse, "and still fewer know how to put into action the knowledge they may already have to become peaceful, positive and prosperous."

Launched during the global economic maelstrom of 2008, Spiritual Money offers a timely step-by-step guide to achieving your personal and financial goals—whatever they might be.

Michelle could certainly afford to offer this book to the world for free. HOWEVER, as she has found, people do not value that which they get for free. And people need to develop a new paradigm for existence. To help them create that, she charges a nominal fee of $11 for the book. If you happen to get this book for free because someone copied it and passed it on to you—realize the more you invest in your own improvement, the more you will actually improve.

Barbara Sleeper, PMP

Acknowledgments

I would like to thank the irresponsible leadership of the United States government at the beginning of the new millennium for motivating me to make this book available to the world. I would also like to thank the financial institutions for never once supporting me or my business efforts so that I had to create a much more effective approach for long-term sustainable success.

Special thanks goes to Liz, my financial planner, for helping me understand how my practices were helping me become so successful. A number of people helped edit this book—Mary, Barb, and Carey. And honorary mention goes to Barbara S. and Judy who helped me bring this book to the final publishing stage in Cheetah speed. Thanks also to my technology team—Shari, Adam, and Kristen for setting this up to sell in a variety of formats. Thank you to Jody for pushing this to publication. And a big thank you to Rita who never ceases to amaze me in what she can accomplish in one day.

Finally, I would like to thank all my customers, suppliers, vendors, contractors, and employees for making my business possible. Most of all, I would like to thank my family and friends for their unwavering support of my efforts and for always believing in me.

Spiritual Money™
Seven Truths that Will Set You Free

Table of Contents

Introduction
Allow the Camel to Pass Through the Eye of the Needle

I've always been interested in money. Like most kids, I suppose, it started when I was around seven or eight years old. I loved to figure out ways to make it, had a great time spending it, became stressed about not having "enough," got competitive in wanting to make more than my brothers, enjoyed sharing it with my friends, became jealous of people who had money when I did not, watched in disbelief as differences in perceptions about money pulled my marriage apart, experienced how it brought out the best and the worst in people, and ultimately learned how irrelevant it was to achieving my goals. Basically, I experienced the truths of money just by living my life.

But let's back up. I was raised middle class. My parents—both public school teachers—worked hard to provide my four brothers, sister and me with all the basics. They performed quite the financial juggling act. By the time I was in college, there were five of us pursuing degrees at the same time.

I was also raised Catholic, so I heard things in church like "money is the root of all evil" and "it's easier for a camel to pass through the eye of the needle than for a rich man to go to heaven."

During my very middle class, Catholic childhood, I heard and experienced some of the common myths about the scarcity of money. I was also raised to believe that I could have anything that I wanted, and could make myself into anyone I wanted to be. But I was the one who had to make it happen. It was never about the money. It was about the drive and the desire to reach my goals, whatever they might be.

Today, as a successful entrepreneur, I realize that there are Seven Spiritual Truths about money. I have experienced them time and time again. In fact, when I really started to pay attention to these Seven Spiritual Truths, I began to notice that I always had as much money as I needed for anything that I wanted to have—or be.

The Seven Spiritual Truths:

1. Money has any meaning you assign it.
2. Goals create money.
3. God helps those who help others.
4. Your financial commitments craft your existence.
5. Money needs to flow.
6. Paying it forward improves cash flow.
7. Wealth is a state of mind.
8. Why are these truths spiritual?

Spirituality is about finding a personal connection in life that gives meaning to your existence. Today, money is part of our existence. The Seven Spiritual Truths helped me make peace with money. Understanding these truths dramatically improved my concept of reality—regardless of whether I had a lot of money or none at all.

Why are these "truths"?

These seven statements, or truths, summarize experiences I've had over and over again with respect to money. They also resonate as truths for many other people. After all, what is a truth other than a widely shared experience that corresponds to a generally agreed upon perception of reality? I'm quite sure other people may experience different realities, and therefore, some of these statements may, in fact, not be truths for them. But these truths have worked for me, and for many others, in creating a happy, fulfilling, and abundant life. They might even work for you.

Why did I create this guide?

I created this guide, along with the exercises in each chapter, to help you experience your own spiritual truths about money. Your dreams and aspirations with respect to money are completely within your reach. I firmly believe, and have experienced countless times, that when you come up with a goal, a dream, or an aspiration, you also have within you the very skills and tools you need to reach it. This set of spiritual truths about money and the accompanying exercises can be part of your personal toolkit to reach your goals.

As you read Spiritual Money, open your mind to this new way of looking at money—and yourself! I hope the entrepreneurial and financial experiences I share with you will help you feel more connected to your own life experiences and empower you to pursue your own dreams and goals as you learn the Seven Spiritual Truths about money.

Michelle LaBrosse, PMP

"Happiness is not in the mere possession of money;
it lies in the joy of achievement, in the thrill of creative effort."

Franklin Delano Roosevelt

Chapter 1

Spiritual Truth #1:
Money Has Any Meaning You Assign It

Money is a medium for us to trade goods and services with each other. Most of us never even see our money. We deposit checks into the bank or have our paycheck directly deposited into our bank accounts, and we make payments by automatic electronic fund transfers or checks. We assign to money our own value, feelings, and perceptions surrounding it.

Before the electronic age, people literally saw more of their money. Now, it's very rare to see even a small percentage of our money—it's becoming even more of an abstraction. Whether your money exists as coins clinking in your purse, bills crumpled in your pocket, wads folded neatly in your wallet, or bits and bytes traveling through the ether, it only has value because of our collective agreement as a society that it has value.

Along with this collective agreement of the value of money, people also assign tremendous meaning and emotion to money. To some, money is energy. To others, having more money means having more power. Some people feel that if someone else gives them money, then they owe that other person something. Some people feel wealthy living below the government mandated poverty line—others, who have hundreds of thousands, even millions, in the bank, feel like they don't have enough.

The following four exercises have helped me to understand the first spiritual truth: That money takes on whatever meaning you assign to it. Once I really "got" this truth, I realized that the meanings I had assigned to money were controlling my emotional responses to it. Once I got a handle on my emotions associated with money, I got a handle on getting as much money as I needed to do whatever it was I wanted to do.

The exercises in this chapter include:

✓ **Exercise 1.1: What does money mean to you?** Take your own inventory.

✓ **Exercise 1.2: What does money mean to others?** Observe reactions to money.

Exercise 1.3: How far will I go? Find the amount of money that is comfortable for you.

Exercise 1.4: Thanksgiving. Learn to be grateful for your gifts

Exercise 1.1: What does money mean to you?

Make a list of what money means to you.

Money means _____

_____

_____

_____

_____

_____

_____

_____

I asked a number of people what money means to them. For most, money represents freedom, comfort, choice, stability, security, fun, influence, power, and sometimes, scarcity.

My personal journey

For me, money is about freedom, influence, creativity, and love, for the following reasons:

Freedom—With an adequate amount of money I feel free to pursue my business goals.

Influence—When I have money, I can give more away to help the causes I believe in.

Creativity—I've had to get very creative at times to generate the resources, and money, needed to pursue my many goals.

Love—I absolutely love money and how it enables my creative expression. ◆

Why perform this exercise?

You may unconsciously be sabotaging yourself with respect to your feelings about money. Because you are naturally attracted to those things that you love, you'll have a more difficult time accepting the money that does come into your life if you hate or fear it.

Exercise 1.2: What does money mean to others?

Walk up to someone you know, or to a complete stranger, and give them whatever amount of money feels comfortable to you. What happened? How did you feel? Why? How did they feel?

When you perform this exercise, make sure it is a spontaneous act and not an act of charity. That is a different exercise.

My personal journey

I first heard about this idea from a friend visiting for the weekend who had read about it in an e-mail message on the Internet. The following Monday I tried it out with my children's after-school sitter. When I went to pick up the children, I handed her a five-dollar bill. Of course, she asked me "What's this for?" I told her about the visit from my friend over the weekend and how we had talked about people's perceptions about money. I told her that I was just giving it to her for no reason.

For the next six months we kept swapping fives, tens, and sometimes twenties. I've also done this a number of times in other situations. For example, I've picked up someone's grocery bill, or covered the toll of the person behind me. I'm usually quite amused because people always think I have a hidden agenda—that I want something from them. ◆

Why perform this exercise?

People are very closed down with respect to money. In today's society, it's considered very impolite to ask about someone's income, or to share your own salary with friends and family. It seems we're all scared in some way that if the "big secret" of our income is generally known, people will either try to take advantage of us if we make too much or will think less of us if we don't make enough. By crossing certain boundaries with the way you share money, you can start to expand your own personal meanings about money.

Exercise 1.3: How far will I go?

Write down how much money you make each month. Now

double that amount. How do you feel? Keep doubling the amount until you feel like you're making enough money for you. What does this final amount mean to you? How would you feel if you were making this amount of money every month right now?

My personal journey

I first read about a variation of this exercise in a book called "The Complete Idiot's Guide to Making Money Through Intuition." I found this book at a store called "Ocean State Job Lots," a store that purchases surplus stock and sells it at deeply discounted rates. The book cost me $3.99. I did every exercise in the book over a two-month period. At this time in my life, money was in short supply. I was in the deep realms of experiencing the "truth" about money. To say that this book was timely is an understatement. Within a year, I went from having no cash, to seeing cash literally fly in the window from a whole variety of sources. Today my business literally generates more cash then the GNP of some developing nations!

This exercise was one of the more illuminating ones, allowing me to realize how much money I needed to feel like I was making enough. I reached my goal of having "enough" within three years of doing this exercise. Now the real fun has begun as I continue to push the financial envelope just to see what happens next. ◆

Why perform this exercise?

You may never have stopped to figure out how much monthly income would make you feel like you were making enough. Or if you did, your internal voice may have said: "Be realistic! How are you ever going to achieve that?" This exercise is about thinking about how much money is really enough for you. It gives you a chance to see how you would feel with a truly abundant sum of money, whatever your definition of "abundant" and "enough" might be.

Exercise 1.4: Thanksgiving

The next exercise is an exercise in gratitude. List all of the things in your life for which you are grateful. Once you've listed them, analyze the themes. Are they about your family, your relationships, your possessions, your experiences, or something else? How many are about money?

Money takes on any meaning you assign to it. You might as well consciously assign positive attributes to money instead of negative ones. By doing so, you can make money work in your favor, as a force for goodness rather than as one that drags you down.

Create your own positive affirmations about money. The key to creating positive affirmations is to keep them upbeat. Instead of saying "I never worry about money," say "I am at peace with how much money effortlessly flows into my life," or "I easily generate the money I need to reach my goals," etc. Repeat these positive affirmations to yourself hundreds of times during the day and especially right before you go to sleep. This will help shift your internal dialog about money.

My personal journey

I've kept a gratitude journal for ten years now. Every night before I go to sleep, I record in my gratitude journal my unique gifts that I've shared with the world that day, and what I want to share with the world tomorrow. I record my short-term and long-term goals. Then I list the things for which I am grateful. I end by quieting my mind, and recording in my journal anything that bubbles up. This whole exercise takes me about 15 minutes.

When I started to recognize the things for which I was most grateful, I brought more of them into my life. I realized that if I wanted more money in my life, I had better start being authentically grateful for the money that was already in my life. ◆

Why perform this exercise?

People have many negative feelings about money. They don't have enough to purchase what they want, or they don't have enough to experience their desired reality. They get depressed about bills. They get into arguments with spouses, children, business partners, friends and family about money. Often, people will be grateful for their relationships, their possessions, and their experiences. But instead of celebrating money, they have an undercurrent of resentment towards it. This affects the meanings they assign to money.

Wrap up

If you're interested in making long-term changes in your life to become more successful, consider answering these wrap up questions. Adults learn and remember by reflecting on what they just experienced. If you can attach a positive emotion to an experience, you'll remember it on a deeper, more permanent basis. When learning new skills, if you can figure out ways to immediately apply them, you'll start to make them a habit and begin using them instinctively.

Reflections

Take a few minutes to reflect on what you learned in this section:

1. What did you learn doing these exercises?
2. How did you feel?
3. How can you use this information in your life?

"The least of things with a meaning is worth more in life than the greatest of things without it."

Anonymous

Chapter 2
Spiritual Truth #2: Goals Create Money

Contrary to what you may believe, you have the ability to achieve any goal you like. By setting a goal, you are immediately putting into motion the actions you will need to reach your goal—almost without any conscious effort. The very act of setting the goal helps create the need, and this in turn helps you secure the resources necessary to achieve your goal. In other words, the need will create the resources.

By thinking about and defining your goal, you'll become more aware of the different options and opportunities that can help you reach it. In many instances, these options and opportunities were there all along. You just weren't conscious of them yet because you hadn't set your goal.

My personal journey

I realized this truth at a young age. When I was in high school, I wanted to study aerospace engineering. My parents took me to visit colleges to evaluate aerospace programs. It turned out that the school I wanted to go to was very expensive, and I knew that if I wanted to attend, I'd have to get a scholarship. Before I visited the school, I had received information about an Air Force Scholarship, but I dismissed it. About a month after I visited the school, I received another informational brochure from the Air Force. This time I paid attention. I managed to pay for that first semester with help from my parents, student loans, and a work-study package from the school. By the middle of second semester I was awarded a full Air Force scholarship.

The point is, I initially didn't have the money to attend

---

that school, but my goal created the need, and I found the resources to meet my goal. Now I need to add a caveat here —you may be thinking that I'm a rocket scientist, but I'm not inherently any smarter than the next person. I went into aerospace engineering despite scoring a 35% in mechanical aptitude on a pre-engineering assessment test. I got my share of Cs in high school—even in high school physics. I did get As in some subjects, like mathematics and band, and I did make friends with people easily, so I was able to get good recommendations. I also befriended people at the school where I wanted to attend.

Despite my financial concerns, I stuck with my goal of becoming an aerospace engineer because that was what I wanted to do. The universe provided me with the resources to meet my goal, even though I wasn't born with the innate talent to achieve it. I graduated from that school cum laude, and was selected as the Class Marshall to lead my senior class into graduation. This was all because I went to a school I loved, and I let the universe provide me with the resources needed to achieve my goals. ◆

Note the word "love." Once you get into the full pursuit of a goal, you'll "fall in love"—you'll fall in love with the goal. Mihaly Csikszentmihalyi, author of Flow: The Psychology of Optimal Experience, has done extensive research on happiness. He observed that people are the happiest when they are in the aggressive pursuit of their goals, goals that have intense meaning for them.

The universe will provide everything you need to pursue your goals—especially if you have a great passion for what you are doing. Some people are afraid to reach for the brass ring—to really go after their goals. They've been conditioned to be reasonable, to be "realistic." When someone tells you that you can't achieve a goal, they are telling you that they can't achieve that goal. You can achieve anything you want to achieve.

I've experienced this truth many times throughout my life, as have numerous other people. When someone doesn't pursue his or her goals, it is never about the money. Lack of money is just an excuse. If you have goals that are meaningful to you, you will find the resources needed to achieve those goals.

> *"People are the happiest when they are in the aggressive pursuit of their goals"*

After I realized this truth, I started setting very high goals. It has taken me a little longer to achieve my lofty goals, but I am achieving them. The goal has created the need and the universe has provided me with the resources to help me meet my goal.

As difficult as it is to believe, some people don't allow themselves to dream or to have goals. They were conditioned at a young age to believe that they couldn't get whatever it was that they wanted.

This chapter focuses on six sets of exercises to help you set and reach your goals:

Exercise 2.1: Goal setting. This set of exercises helps you set goals that are meaningful to you.

Exercise 2.2: Planning. The second set of exercises allows you to create plans so that you can work towards achieving your goals.

Exercise 2.3: Your support network. The third set of exercises helps you identify your support network needed to achieve your goals.

Exercise 2.4: Putting out your net. The fourth set of exercises helps you set up your "net" so you can catch the opportunities flying by that will help you reach your goals.

Exercise 2.5: Mastermind. The fifth set of exercises requires two other people to help generate ideas on how to reach your goals.

Exercise 2.6: Moving on. The sixth set of exercises helps you let go of goals that are no longer serving you so you can make room for new goals and new opportunities in your life.

Exercise 2.1: Goal setting

I set short-term goals, long-term goals, professional goals, and personal goals. In my nightly gratitude journal, I set my short-term goals. These are goals that I want to achieve within one week to one month. Long-term goals may take me six months to three years to accomplish. I set goals about making money. I also set goals that are less specific and more enduring, such as raising happy, self-confident children.

Goal setting helps me focus my attention and to be more aware and open to the opportunities that can help me meet my goals. The first set of exercises focuses on setting your own goals.

Identifying your goals

Identify a goal you have already achieved. What happened that helped you achieve this goal? Did you have all of the resources needed to achieve that goal before you started?

After you set your goal, what resources appeared that you didn't know about before you started?

Why perform this exercise?

Success breeds success. When you identify the ways in which you have already been successful, it will give you the confidence to reach for other goals.

Prioritizing your goals

Identify 25 things you want to do with your life before you die. Once you've identified these 25 things, prioritize them in order of importance to you, then in order of how soon you'd like to accomplish them. Create a reality rating of your current ability to accomplish the things on your list. The reality rating is based on your past performance accomplishing goals, your current motivation to achieve them, and the current external influences on your life, such as young children, aging parents, divorce, or health issues.

Why perform this exercise?

A list of 25 goals is a real stretch for most people. By listing this many goals, and then prioritizing them, you will get a much better sense of what is important to you right now.

My personal journey

I performed this exercise a couple of months before purchasing lake-front property when I had two toddlers at home and was essentially a stay-at-home mom pulling in less than $30k income per year. Through this exercise I realized how important it was for me to pursue my dream of building a house on a lake. ◆

Starting your goal journal

Start your own goal journal. Identify your short-term, long-term, professional, and personal goals. Get as creative as you want with this. Draw or paste in pictures of what you'd like to achieve. Perform a "backwards from perfect" exercise—pretend you've already reached your goals and record how you're feeling and what happened that helped you reach them. Make up a song about how great you are that you've achieved your goals. Review your goals however many times you'd like. Some people like to review their goals more frequently than others. I've noticed that after a few months, I'll go back and look at my goal journal, and be surprised at how often I've achieved what I set in motion just a few months earlier.

Why perform this exercise?

Articulating your goals by writing them down or sharing them with others helps make them real. Reviewing your goals periodically can be re-affirming and can help redirect your activities to help you get back on the track achieving goals that are important to you. This helps give meaning to your life.

Exercise 2.2: Planning

Besides setting my goals, I also develop plans that help me reach them. A goal without action is just a dream, and action without any direction will get you nowhere—fast.

A project is any unique and temporary endeavor. This is what goals are—they are your projects. Goals are typically unique and they are temporary. Once you've reached your goal, you set up new ones.

Planning is vital to achieve your goals. I use the exercise I call "From Vision to Action" to map out the route to achieve my goals. Sometimes I am clear about the steps I need to take to reach my goals. Other times I need to wait for the directions to appear.

With this approach, you have to be comfortable with ambiguity and uncertainty. It also helps to have an unwavering faith in the possible. If one route isn't getting you where you want to go, patiently wait and listen. Keep yourself open and aware of signs indicating the route that will take you there.

This approach works well when you break your goal down into smaller goals. The "milestones"—the mile markers of your goal—will be close together. If you make a wrong turn or hit a dead end in your attempt to reach a goal, you won't be too far off the right path.

And later successes are built on earlier successes. When you experience how your goals really do create needs that the universe helps fill, you can let go and trust that the universe will help you in other areas when you need resources to meet new goals. Your plan can illuminate these areas for you.

In this second exercise, you create your plans to help you reach your goals.

From vision to action—creating your plan

The first part of a plan in project management is called your "work break down structure." Your overall goal is the main "deliverable" of your project. From this deliverable, you identify sub-deliverables that are necessary to reach the overall goal. For each sub-deliverable, you have a series of tasks that you must perform in order to create that particular deliverable. To illustrate this process, I'll show you how I accomplished my goal of writing this book.

Goal: Help Liz get more financial planning customers by sharing my experience of increasing my net worth more than ten fold in less than six months.

Table 2.1 *shows the work break down structure for a sample project, or plan:*

Training Material • Write draft of work book • Edit draft of work book
Course Preparation • Select date for course • Identify target market for course • Create promotional material for target market • Reserve venue for course • Create website and web registration module for course • Place advertisements for course in publications viewed by target market
Course Delivery • Practice course to ensure people learn through their participation • Manage the course venue to ensure participants are well cared for and the environment is conducive to learning
Introduce Liz and share her role in my success
Get feedback from participants to ensure they learned the material presented
Lessons Learned • Identify what worked and what didn't work • Make modifications as needed • Assess next steps

Table 2.1: Work break down structure of a plan

Why perform this exercise?

Vision without action is just dreaming. Action without a vision of where you're heading is just time wasted spinning your wheels. People who achieve their goals and dreams know that just having an idea is a very small part of turning the idea into reality. Creating step-by-step plans makes it much easier to take focused and aligned action every day that will lead toward the fulfillment of your goals and dreams.

Getting more detailed

Once you have your work break down structure in place, then you can create your project plan that outlines:

- How long you think these tasks will take you.

- When you will complete these tasks.

- Who will help you to complete these tasks?

Using this model, create a plan for one of the goals you identified in Exercise 2.1 on goal setting.

Why perform this exercise?

Instead of leaving the pursuit of your dreams to chance, taking action in a set of coordinated steps can help you achieve goals. Many people wait before they pursue their dreams until they have everything in order, or they say they will go after a dream if they achieve another thing first, for example, winning the lottery. There is no reason to put your goals on the back burner while waiting for that "someday" windfall to appear if you create and implement a well-thought-out plan. You'll acquire the resources to achieve any goal you decide to go after, just by putting in motion the steps you need to take to reach your goals.

Table 2.2 *shows a sample project plan:*

Task	Duration	Deadline	Who
Training Material: • Write Draft • Edit Draft	2 Weeks 2 Weeks	May 1 May 15	Michelle, Jean, Liz Mary, Liz
Course Preparation: • Select Date • Identify Target Market • Create Promos • Reserve Venue • Create Web System • Place Ads	1 day 5 days 2 weeks 1 day 1 day 2 days	May 1 May 1 May 7 May 1 May 15 May 15	Liz, Michelle Liz, Michelle Michelle, Jeff Liz Michelle Liz, Michelle
Course Delivery: • Practice Course • Manage Venue	1 Day 1 Day	June 1 June 15	Michelle, Jean, Liz Jean, Liz
Introduce Liz	15 Minutes	June 15	Michelle
Get feedback	2 Days	June 30	Pam
Lessons Learned: • Identify Effectiveness • Make Modifications • Assess Next Steps	1 day 1 day 1 day	June 30 July 7 July 7	Michelle, Liz, Pam, Jean Liz, Michelle Liz, Michelle

Table 2.2: Sample project plan

My personal journey

For a short period of time when I was setting up my current company, I worked with a guy named Peter. Peter struggled to formulate a plan with me to get my business off the ground because he claimed we didn't have enough money to do what he wanted to do. I stopped working with Peter, put my own plan into action, and over the next eight months I found all the resources I needed to get my company going. Today, I'm incredibly grateful that I didn't have the type of money Peter needed to get my business off the ground. Now the company is built on a solid foundation of accelerated training products that are truly needed in the marketplace. ◆

Exercise 2.3: Your support network

People need other people to help them reach their goals. We all have people already in our lives who could, in some way, support the pursuit of our dreams. We also all have people in our lives who don't believe in themselves and therefore certainly wouldn't believe in us. And there are always new people coming in and out of our lives—some of whom are sent to us in order to help us reach our goals or who we are supposed to help in reaching their goals.

The third exercise is an assessment of your own personal network. Believe it or not, we all have about 150 people in each of our own individual networks. In the following exercises, you'll draw pictures of your network and understand how it can both help and hinder you in the pursuit of your goals.

Your own personal network

In this exercise, you'll need a large piece of paper and a pen or pencil. Draw a circle in the middle of the paper, which signifies you. Then draw circles all around you, which signify all of the people around you in your network, personal or professional. Write the name of each person in every circle. The closer the circle is to you, the more day-to-day contact you have with that person. The bigger influence someone has on you, the bigger his or her circle will be. Put a "+" or a "-" next to each circle to indicate whether this person has a positive or a negative influence on you. It might be hard to identify your 150 people in one sitting, so do this exercise over time. Come back to it as you remember more people in your network. Once you're done, you'll get a sense of how many positive ("+") people are in your life and how many negative ("-") people are in your life.

Example:

+

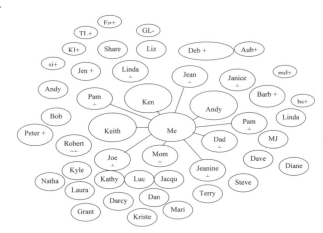

Why perform this exercise?

In order to reach your goals, you need to either minimize your interactions with the negative people that surround you, or reduce their negative influence. You can do this by increasing your interactions with the positive people in your life, thereby increasing the effectiveness of their positive influence. You may also find that there are those in your life right under your nose who can help you to reach your goals, or who may need help in reaching one of their goals.

Your inner circle

Choose one of your bigger goals. Using your support network diagram, draw an inner circle of people whom you could help in achieving their goals. By helping them with their goals, you'll in fact be helping yourself to achieve your goals.

Why perform this exercise?

One person has the power to change his or her life. Groups of people have the power to change the world. We all exist on this planet together to help one other. By helping others, you help yourself, and by allowing others to help you, you are in fact helping them. Many other people may have already achieved the goal you are setting out to achieve. By seeking out these people, you can gain valuable insight into achieving your goals.

Exercise 2.4: Putting out your net

In putting out your net, you'll get what you need in order to reach your goal. When you were creating your plan in Exercise 2.2, you most likely ran into areas where you knew you needed something to be done—a missing element. The universe will provide these missing elements for you. But you must have an idea of what they are first so that when they come into your life you know what they are.

My personal journey

I'm always on the lookout for people or opportunities to help me reach my goals. And I find some of them in the most interesting places. I moved from Washington State to Connecticut and was having a problem making friends. Therefore, one of my personal goals at that time was to make more friends. I also wanted to learn yoga to enhance some accelerated learning principles I was testing. I signed up for a week-long yoga class, and met Liz within the first ten minutes of the first class. By the end of the class, I had a new friend and a new financial planner. The need created the opportunity.

Another time, I needed to put together a Public Relations team. I was just starting my research when, out of the blue, a company sent me an e-mail message introducing their Public Relations company designed for successful start-ups. When I needed someone to help me take care of my children, my dog escaped and was returned by a 21-year-old woman who was recently fired from her job and had been a nanny a couple of years ago.

Once again, the need created the opportunity.

This next exercise is to help open up your awareness to what you need. Take one of your goals as an example, and make a few lists to include the following information:

- Identify your goal and why you want to achieve it.
- List the actions you can take yourself to achieve the goal.
- List what help you'll need from others to achieve your goal.

Table 2.3 will help you identify your goal, what you will need to do to achieve it, and whether or not you will need any help.

Why perform this exercise?

Don't let "missing links" prevent you from pursuing your goals. When you identify what you will need to accomplish a goal, the resources will begin to appear.

Exercise 2.5: Mastermind

Find two people who want to do this activity with you. You can do this with just one other person, but you'll generate far more ideas and energy with two. However, if more than two people want to join you, resist the temptation to include more people, as the feedback gets too diffuse if you have more than three people in a group.

The purpose of this exercise is to create collective stories about how each of you reaches your goals. Begin by having each person identify three goals. Then have everyone else make up stories about how that individual achieved their goals as if they had already happened.

1. All three people get centered and calm. When I participate in a mastermind session, we all do pryana breathing and the yoga sun salutation to relax.

2. One person states his/her three goals. The other two people make up stories about how that individual has already achieved those goals, being as creative and descriptive as possible. One at a time, each person weaves a tale while the other two people listen with 100% attention to the story. The "folklore" is that by having all three people focus on the story, more energy is put out into the universe to make it a reality. My

Goal	Why do you want to achieve this goal?	What actions can you take to achieve this goal?	What help, if any, do you need in order to achieve this goal?

Table 2.3: Defining and analyzing your goals

theory is that you'll hear better if you give the story teller your undivided attention, and this will help you visualize opportunities to reach your goals that you may not have thought of before.

3. The next person states three goals—the other two people make up stories about that person's goals.

4. The last person states three goals—the other two people make up stories about that person's goals.

Why perform this exercise?

The first reason to do this exercise is because it's fun. It's also really motivating. If you do anything on a set schedule, then over time, you will become accountable for sticking with your goal long enough to see it through to fruition.

Exercise 2.6: Moving on

By setting goals and developing plans to achieve your goals, you create the resources (including money) needed to achieve whatever you set your mind to. Once you successfully achieve your initial goals, you will be motivated to set new goals. The goals and aspirations that you had at 15 are going to be different than the ones you have at 25, at 35, at 45 and so on. Just because you've achieved a goal doesn't mean you're "stuck" with the results. Once you experience what you wanted to experience and begin to feel like it's time to move on, it probably is. If you're no longer "in love" with what it is you are doing, by all means start the goal-setting process again.

There is a saying that you should work to live instead of living to work. That really depends on how you define work. If you view work as something you have to do to make money, then you are not doing the right thing for you at this stage of your life. You can make a substantial living by doing what you love. And "what you love" will change throughout your life. If you're dissatisfied with what you are currently doing and are stuck "living to work"—then consider moving on.

Complaints lead to commitments. If you're very dissatisfied about something in your life right now, then that is the area where you can set some new goals to move away from it. In our creativity class we have an exercise called from Complaints to Commitments. If you're ready to move on from one success to experience another aspect of life, this exercise will help you move from the complaining stage to the commitment stage.

This exercise shows you how to hatch creative ideas from the energy and awareness behind problems to discover what is truly important to you. Behind every complaint is a deep-felt commitment to do something. Without the commitment there would be no complaint. It is the commitment that you care about and gives you energy and direction

Creating is about bringing forth something from nothing because you love it so much you want it to exist. When you deeply value something and are committed to creating it in your life, you will begin to repeatedly complain around not having it. Find your strongest complaints and you will discover your deepest commitments.

1) On this worksheet are two columns. The left column is for your complaints and the right column is for your commitments. In the left column, list your ten biggest complaints in your life right now.

Complaints	Commitments

2) Convert your complaints into commitments. Ask yourself what it is that you care so much about that when you fall short of achieving it or expressing it, you feel like complaining.

3) Now list these commitments on the right side of the worksheet. Check and make sure that every item is something positive. This list should capture many of the things you care most about in your life.

4) The last step is to look at each commitment and set an achievable goal that expresses that commitment.

Why perform this exercise?

This is not a dress rehearsal for your life, it IS your life. If a goal you worked so hard to achieve is not what you want to do anymore, you have to give yourself permission to move on.

Wrap up

Goal setting is a life-long process. Most things usually work out for the best, but when you're in the thick of things, sometimes that's hard to remember. The approach taken in this chapter may at first seem contradictory: Set your goals and make plans to achieve your dreams while having the faith that you will get what you need to accomplish them. These concepts can and do work very well together. It's as if you are the architect and the universe is the contractor. What I've learned is that things always work out for the best. Even with the best laid plans, things will and do go awry— but there usually is a silver lining.

Reflections

Take a few minutes to reflect on these exercises:

1. What did you learn doing these exercises?

2. How did you feel?

3. How can you use this information in your life?

*"We must walk consciously only part way toward our goal,
and then leap in the dark to our success."*

Henry David Thoreau

Chapter 3
Spiritual Truth # 3: God Helps Those Who Help Others

I heard a variation of this throughout my childhood: "God helps those who help themselves." As I got older, and started studying comparative religions, I learned about karma. What I learned about karma is that the universe basically runs a balance sheet. If you do bad things to people, bad things will happen to you. If you are helpful to others and do good things, other people will be helpful to you and good things will happen. This is a very simplistic definition of karma, but it has served me well. If you apply this definition to money, you'll find that the best way to make more money is to help other people make more money.

> *"The best way to make more money is to help other people make more money"*

I've been running my own business for almost two decades now. I started my first company when I was 25 years old and just out of the Air Force. I learned in the first three months that in order to make money I had to help other people make money. It wasn't good enough that I was technically talented in my field. If I couldn't help other people make money, no one would hire me. I created a program that taught defense contractors how to win Air Force contracts, and away I went. I made more money in three months than I did the previous three years as an Air Force officer.

Now I apply this truth to every aspect of my life. With every interaction I have with others, I try to figure out how we can both win through the association. It may or may not be about making money. I also help people with no strings attached. It increases the positive column on my balance sheet with the universe. I don't always get an immediate "return on investment" with my benevolence, but I get remunerated in a variety of other ways. It just improves the overall quality of my life to help others. You get what you give. If you want to make lots of money, you have to give lots of money and give lots of people a lot of ways to make money.

This chapter focuses on five exercises designed to make you aware of opportunities that allow you to be helpful and to be helped. They are:

Exercise 3.1: Get rid of your blockages and become more helpful

Exercise 3.2: Find the right opportunities to be helpful

Exercise 3.3: Develop an attitude of gratitude

Exercise 3.4: Allow others to help you

Exercise 3.5: Grow flowers from weeds—adversity and opportunity are twins

Exercise 3.1: Get rid of your blockages and become more helpful

Anger and its supporting actor, fear, along with jealousy, self-righteous indignation, complacency, apathy, busyness, and self-involvement—are emotions and situations that block us from helping others. They, in turn, block us from accepting help from others into our lives. If you have blockages that prevent you from being helpful, you'll also have blockages with respect to accepting money into your life. There are no discontinuities in life. You get what you give. You reap what you sow.

My personal journey

I went through a very tough period in my life when I was forced out of a job. I had relocated my family across the country because the company that hired me made a commitment to have me on staff for five years but disbanded my department 18 months into the position. When I left that job, my ex-husband filed a lawsuit against me to pick up the cost of our children's health insurance (at the time he was also only covering about half of the required child support). I was very angry, afraid of how I was going to make a living, hurt about how I let myself get trapped in the no-win employment situation, angry at my ex-husband for kicking me when I was down, and annoyed with how the people who hired me were only concerned about saving their own skin and did not offer me any help. Basically, I was in a full-blown, "poor me" blame game. Looking back on the whole situation now, I can honestly say that losing that job and dealing with the ensuing adversity was the best thing that ever happened to me. I started my current company, became much more compassionate to the plight of others, learned how to live happily on very little money, and learned that moving on doesn't just mean forgiveness— it means acceptance. What prompted the shift in my outlook was a firm commitment to focus on the future. Yes, I could have pursued a labor lawsuit against my former employer for breach of contract. I had a good case and may have been successful, but at what cost? I decided that it was not my job to right the "injustices" I experienced at the hands of this major conglomerate—which, by the way, has since suffered more major losses—(karma!). Instead, I decided I did not want to divert my energy to the past or in any negative direction. I opted to move on. ◆

Reflect upon your life over the past week, month, year, or decade and identify instances when you were not helpful to others. Were there times when, in fact, you may have gone out of your way to be hurtful? Why was this going on? How were you feeling at the time? What lesions did you learn from this experience? If you did move on from that time hurtful time in your life, what prompted it?

Why perform this exercise?

We all have our own personal trials and tough times. When you reflect on the hard times you've experienced—and survived—it makes the next set of problems a little easier to weather because you know that this too shall pass. You know you can transcend any hard time with grace and compassion.

Exercise 3.2: Find the right opportunities to be helpful

There are an infinite number of ways you can be helpful. It can be a genuine way of living your life and moving throughout the world. Being helpful can be as simple as being kind or as all-encompassing as giving up all your free time to champion causes such as animal rights or fighting homelessness, hunger, poverty and diseases in undeveloped countries. I've also learned that sometimes being helpful can actually end up having the opposite effect— especially if it comes at the expense of hurting yourself.

Brainstorm all the opportunities you have to be helpful in your personal and professional life. It will probably take you about five to ten minutes to come up with examples. Once you're done, record how you feel about each opportunity. If it feels right, then consider doing it. If it doesn't feel right, or if you pursue some of these opportunities and they stop being right for you, then give yourself permission to move on. I've learned that if you're going to be helpful, it has to be the right situation.

Opportunity to be Helpful	Gut Feeling About Opportunity

Why perform this exercise?

There are an infinite number of ways to be helpful. When you identify the best ways for you to contribute, and in which situations, then it is easier to say no to people who ask for help in situations that are just not right for you. Then it's the "I already gave at the office" response until a better opportunity comes along.

Exercise 3.3: Develop an attitude of gratitude

When other people help you, it is absolutely crucial that you are truly thankful for their help. Review situations over the past week where people have helped you—service people in stores, restaurants, your children's teachers, the clerk in the grocery store, etc. Reflect on your interaction with them. Did you approach each situation with an attitude of gratitude for their help? Look at your interactions with people today. Remember to thank them for their help—even if you are paying them, they are still helping you. Evaluate other ways you can thank them that goes beyond the simple thank you—a note, flowers, or a note to their boss acknowledging their helpful demeanor.

Why perform this exercise?

Taking the time to acknowledge and appreciate other people will actually get you even better service in the future. Think about it—wouldn't you much rather help someone who was kind, friendly and appreciative, versus someone who only complained that you didn't do enough for them when you did help them?

My personal journey

You just never know what other people are going through. We tend to judge ourselves by our intentions. We judge others by observing their actions, and then base our perception of their intentions by their actions. For example, just recently I had ordered a major piece of equipment for my pool. I wanted to have it installed by Memorial Day weekend and thought I had ordered it in plenty of time.

Well, the days kept slipping by. Usually I go by the adage

that the squeaky wheel gets the grease, but for some reason my gut was telling me to hold back. Sure enough, when the supplier called me, she explained that she had been in the hospital with a serious illness and internal bleeding. She was part of a small family business and this was their busy season. Not only were they worried about their family member, they had to service some very demanding clients who also wanted their pools opened by Memorial Day weekend. Fortunately, my supplier and I now get phenomenal service from this company. ◆

Exercise 3.4: Allow others to help you

When I first learned how to sell, I realized that for people to like you (and therefore want to purchase anything at all from you) you have to let them be helpful. People have an innate desire to help other people. What I learned while in sales training was that people actually liked me more if I let them help me than if I did something to help them. Again, this situation has to follow the same rhythms as when you help other people—it must be authentic, and done in the right time and context.

You have to learn to listen to your intuition about people who want to help. Sometimes people who seem to want to help you really may not be there to help you at all. For example, predatory telemarketers who prey on lonely people are one subset of humanity that has ulterior motives.

Learn to understand your responses. When you are in need of help from someone else, you are usually putting "vibes" out into the universe that other people sense. When people appear to help you, do you accept their help, or do you avoid their help because of past conditioning? If you didn't put out the "I need help" vibe, and someone appears who wants to help you, listen to your intuition when it tells you to tread carefully. Learn to distinguish the difference between the feeling of hesitation from past conditioning and your intuition telling you that the situation is not right for you.

Identify one area in your life where you could use some help, right now. Identify at least ten ways that the universe might be able to provide that help for you. It seems that sometimes help comes from the least likely places and you just need to be open to receiving it. You may get stuck here—if so, give the exercise some time to incubate and then come back to it. You might start to notice that help arrives as soon as you put it out there that you need help. If you find yourself getting stuck, identify why you need the help you're requesting.

My personal journey

At this point in time, I could use some help in selling out my new courses. The ways the universe could help me would be to:

- Send more customers my way

- Give me inspiration to modify my marketing message so it's more captivating to my target audience

- Set up alliances with larger corporations who need this training

- Make sure I am ready to handle that level of business

- Get people to license the course in areas with the greatest demand

- Provide promotional opportunities

I need the help in order to grow the business with new product lines and to provide for long-term stability for my employees and myself. To accomplish this I need to increase the profitability of the existing product lines.

Some solutions I came up with:

- Get companies who choose us as their preferred training provider and put all their people through our public programs

- Get alliances for the other product lines so it doesn't require so much investment capital

- Get referrals from past students

- Make it easy for people to register

If you get stuck again, look more closely at your reasons for needing help, and ask "why." For example, in my case, why do I want long-term stability for my employees and myself? Answer: Because we all have dependent children and we need to create stable nests from which they will launch themselves out into the world. It is our time to become the "prudential" in their lives.

There is another factor to consider when letting other people help you—their competence. If they don't know what they are doing, they can, in fact, do more harm than good. And sometimes help comes with a cost attached, which is entirely appropriate and necessary for the help you are going to receive.

Since this is a book about money, I will mention that there are many people out there who can help you with money— they are called "financial advisors." I found my financial advisor in my yoga class. I needed one and she appeared.

I was open to having that type of help in my life at the time. I didn't just immediately jump at the chance to have her become my financial advisor. Our relationship evolved over time as I got to know her better and we developed a level of trust and understanding regarding my goals and her capabilities to advise me in the pursuit of my goals.

You need to pursue your helping relationships the same way. Get to know people on a personal level. Are you comfortable with them? Does it feel right to you? Do you feel they have your best interests in mind? Trust your gut instincts when you are letting people into your life to help you—whether they are helping you for a fee or helping you out of the goodness of their heart.

Trust your gut, but also do your homework. In terms of financial advisors, check out their credentials, go to one of their seminars, and understand how they get paid.

Why perform this exercise?

Some of us are very conditioned to do it all ourselves, to be independent, and to take care of our own. But we're all on this planet together and live an interdependent existence. If you don't agree with this, just think about all the people who were involved in enabling you to eat breakfast this morning—the dairy farmer, the baking company, the distribution companies, the shipping companies, the grocer, the banking professionals who help transact all the business, the refrigerator manufacturer, the electric company, the dish manufacturers, the silverware manufacturers, etc. Everyone needs to be needed, and by learning how to let others help you, you are helping them.

Exercise 3.5: Grow flowers from weeds—adversity and opportunity are twins

When you're down on your luck, the best thing you can do to get things flowing in your life again is to go out and help someone else. This can be in the form of financial help as in simply writing a check to someone who needs money, donating time to a cause you believe in, or in just viewing a situation from a different angle and turning it into an opportunity.

Identify a situation in your life right now that isn't working. Figure out ways that you could turn that situation into an opportunity by being helpful.

Why perform this exercise?

Events and situations are neither negative nor positive—they just are. We put our own spin on them. If you can spin them into an opportunity, you will truly live a blessed, abundant existence. Challenges will come up in your life, as they do in everyone's life, and if you take them with a positive attitude they will look like a great series of serendipitous opportunities.

My personal journey

I put one of my good friends into a job where she was in over her head. I had her working as a trainer in my company. She was setting up my first training center, and because she was an accountant, I also had her closing the books at the year's end. The job of closing the books was a nightmare and she ended up spending over 100 hours on it before I realized that I had put her in a very difficult position. I found another way to do the job, but she still sent me a bill for $7500. I almost choked when I saw what she wanted for the job—and it still hadn't been completed. I realized that I had a choice in how I responded. I could have reacted in my standard way, which is flight—(I don't like to fight)—meaning that I would have totally backed out of the relationship. This would have left me with the other requirement of finding someone to do the training and help me get the training center going. I decided to try something different. I looked at ways we could increase enrollment in her classes as a way of covering her bill and I also enlisted her help working with me to increase the number of students in her classes. In this way, we both benefited from the outcome, and no one was hurt or left feeling frustrated or angry. ◆

Wrap up

All aspects of life can be a tremendous adventure or simply something you endure. You create the reality. If you think people are nasty and negative, that is what you'll experience. If you recognize their gifts, they will share them with you. If you look for opportunities to be helpful, you will meet lots of people who are looking for ways to help you. You really do reap what you sow.

Reflections

Take a few moments to reflect on what you learned, felt, and experienced by doing the activities in this chapter. Has it changed the way you plan to interact with people?

54

"You have not lived a perfect day, even though you have earned your money, unless you have done something for someone who will never be able to repay you."

Ruth Smeltzer

Chapter 4

*Spiritual Truth #4: Your Financial Commitments
Craft Your Existence*

You can set up any type of life you want. If you want to live in a nice neighborhood, you'll incur a financial commitment that will impact how you live your life. Even if you have the cash on hand to purchase the house outright, you'll still have the day-to-day upkeep issues of the property. You can do these upkeep tasks yourself (thereby creating the essence of your existence) or you can hire others to do the ongoing upkeep tasks (thereby creating another type of existence). If you want to drive an expensive car, you'll incur a financial commitment that will impact your existence. If you want to send your children to private school, that financial commitment will not only give your children a different existence than public school, but will also introduce you to a different community of people who may dramatically change your existence.

My personal journey

I have experienced this "spiritual truth" after the fact once too often. For example, I built a house on a lake. I had no idea what "existence" I was creating by making this financial commitment. The house I built was beautiful and in the summer I had a lot of company. But in the winter, the place was very isolating. It was a lot of work to keep up the property. What was initially my dream house, over time, felt like the "mistake on the lake." I eventually released myself from the financial commitment of the lake house and changed my existence to a different one I wanted to experience. Now, I carefully define what type of life I want to create and I look at how my financial commitments will either help or hinder that existence. ◆

*There are five exercises in this chapter. The first set helps
you see how your existing financial commitments are
creating your current reality. The next set of activities
helps you consciously create the existence you would like
to experience based on your financial commitments.*

**Exercise 4.1: Identify your current financial
commitments.** In this exercise you establish your current
personal balance sheet—your financial assets and liabilities.

Exercise 4.2: How you feel about your net worth. In this
exercise you understand your emotional reaction to your
balance sheet.

**Exercise 4.3: Identify how your financial commitments
are shaping your reality.** In this exercise you establish
how your past decisions are affecting your current reality
and if they are still serving you.

**Exercise 4.4: Determine what you can do with respect
to your financial commitments to create the type
of life you want.** In this exercise you brainstorm ways
to move from your current existence that is created by
your financial commitments to an existence you'd like to
experience at some point in the future.

**Exercise 4.5: Goals and the financial commitment to
reach them.** In this exercise you pull together the work
you did on setting goals (Chapter 2) and getting the right
type of people to help you reach your financial goals
(Chapter 3), with an understanding of how your financial
commitments affect your existence.

Exercise 4.6: Balancing multiple requirements. In this
exercise you learn how to identify your numerous priorities
and analyze the various options you have to meet those
priorities.

Exercise 4.1: Identify your current financial commitments

We're going to get really practical here. You're going to list your current "assets" and your current "liabilities." This shows your balance sheet.

Why perform this exercise?

You need to know where you are financially in order to develop a map of where you want to go. Everything changes over time, so even if you have done this before, update your numbers now.

Exercise 4.2: How do you feel about this number (your net worth)?

Write down how you feel about this number. If you've done net worth analyses previously, record how you feel about this number now and if it is different than the way you felt about it before. Why do you feel this way about that number? How would you like to feel about this number?

My personal journey

I first did this assessment in my mid-twenties and when I saw my "net worth" number I felt GREAT. I felt on top of the world. Over the ensuing decade, I watched my net worth double then triple into six figures. It kept on growing into my mid-thirties, then wham—I got divorced. Even though I was a very successful career woman, I saw my net worth plummet. It didn't just get cut in half by having my life partner leave me, but over the next five years after my divorce, it plummeted, as did his net worth as well. My finances fell apart as I juggled being a single mom raising two kids on my own while running a company and dealing

---

with the emotional fallout from the divorce. What I learned from all this is that you can't base your self-worth on your net worth. ◆

Exercise 4.1

Assets	Monetary Value
Home Equity	
IRAs	
Roth IRAs	
Brokerage Accounts (stocks/bonds/mutual funds)	
Pension Funds	
401K/403B	
Savings Accounts (All)	
Checking Account	
Intellectual Property (works you've created for which you earn royalties or passive income)	
Cars	
Jewelry	
Other	
Total	

Exercise 4.1 cont.

Liabilities	Monetary Value
Mortgage	
Auto Loans	
Credit Card Debt	
Tuition (current or student loans)	
Other	
Total Liabilities	
Total Assets	
Net Worth (assets-liabilities)	

Why perform this exercise?

As you watch this number fluctuate during your lifetime, you learn that you cannot tie your self-worth to your net worth. If you feel great about your net worth and go around acting really pompous about it, you'll alienate people. If you feel like the scourge of the earth because your net worth isn't what you think it should be, you'll become pathetic. It's only a number and you can assign any feeling you want to it. It doesn't make sense to get emotional about numbers. There are ways you can improve it and a good financial planner can help you create a road map.

Exercise 4.3: Identify how your financial commitments are shaping your reality.

- What is your largest financial commitment?
- How do you feel about it?
- What influenced you to take on that commitment?
- Is it still serving you?

Why perform this exercise?

You can create any type of existence you want, if you're conscious of how your past choices have created your current existence. This exercise will help you become more conscious of how your financial commitments are creating your current reality.

My personal journey

What I learned by experiencing my own personal "stock market" crash was that the commitments I made while I was married were actually depleting my overall balance sheet—not just from a "numbers" perspective either. The financial commitments I had made earlier in a different part of my life were creating an existence I no longer wanted to live. I had built a beautiful house on a little lake in the foothills of the Cascade Mountains outside Seattle, Washington. It took 30 minutes to get into town, and I had to drive into town twice a day because of the children's school. A daily two-hour drive in the car through winding mountain roads creates one heck of a day-in and day-out reality. Living that far off the beaten track made it difficult to run a business and difficult for a newly single mother to even consider striking up any type of personal relationships. In other words, an existence that would have been fine being

> married felt like a prison term being single. My financial
> commitment to that house shaped a reality I no longer
> wanted to experience. ◆

Exercise 4.4: Determine what you can do with respect to
your financial commitments to create the type of life you want.

We all make choices in life. Dreams can become nightmares
and you can move on from aspects of your life you no
longer wish to experience. Or maybe you got diverted
from a long-held dream by "life" itself. Based on what
you discovered in the previous exercise, identify a current
financial commitment that may be holding you back from
fulfilling your current needs. Brainstorm all the possible
ways to move towards a different type of existence. This is
a very free-flowing exercise—write down as many ideas as
possible. You'll build upon these ideas in the next exercise.

Why perform this exercise?

We don't have to be a slave to our past decisions. You
have the power to create any type of existence you want.
Once you start to be more conscious of how your financial
commitments craft your existence, you can begin to
effectively design a new life of your own choosing. This may
mean letting go of financial commitments (huge mortgages,

My personal journey

I eventually sold my lake front house, and put aside my
dreams of running a multi-million dollar company that
enabled millions of people to rapidly reach their goals. I
moved 3,000 miles away, took a job as a research scientist,

> bought a house in a very modest neighborhood three miles
> from my parents' house and started a new life. I loved it.
> My children were able to take the bus to school—no more
> 60-minute commutes twice a day to bring them to school.
> I bought a house less than two miles from my job and
> negotiated flex time/telecommuting with my new employer
> so I still had a great deal of autonomy. To get this, I had to
> give up the financial commitments I had made that were
> creating an existence that no longer worked for me. I made
> new financial commitments and created a new existence. ◆

the credit card debt that is suffocating you, etc) or accepting
a new financial commitment that you hadn't considered
previously.

Exercise 4.5: Goals and the financial commitment to reach
them.

Chapter 2 describes goal setting. The exercises in that
chapter had you explore what you wanted to achieve.
Pick one of the goals you identified. What type of financial
commitment will you have to make to achieve this goal? If
you're unsure of the financial commitment necessary, meet
with the financial advisor you identified in Chapter 3. How
will this create your existence? How do you feel about this
financial commitment?

Why perform this exercise?

You can create any type of reality you want, but these
realities come with a price tag. By understanding the
price tag on what it is you want to experience, you can
assess how important it is to you to experience that reality.
Sometimes the financial commitment that is required to
meet a goal doesn't "feel" right. You know you want to

My personal journey

One of my goals is to raise happy, self-confident children. To do that, I need to make sure that they are happy, and doing well in school. One of my children was in a school that was just not the right fit for her. We did an analysis of all her requirements and then looked at our various options. The number one option to help her meet her requirements (balanced with the requirements of my other child and myself) was to help her find a private school with a low student-to-teacher ratio, a lot of one-on-one attention from the teachers and staff at the school, and an opportunity for her to play sports in a non-competitive environment. As with most things, once we were clear about what we wanted, we quickly found a school that met our requirements. Within one month, we had her happily situated in her new school.

For those of you who have taken on the commitment of private school, you know the financial commitment. The tuition was a significant part of my take home salary. But I created a much nicer existence for both my child and myself. I enjoyed the parents who were also aligned with similar educational goals as my own, and I made a number of new friends because of this financial commitment. The commitment was based on the overall goal I had to raise happy and self-confident children. At the same time, it did craft an elemental part of my day-to-day existence. ◆

pursue the goal, but "advisors" are telling you that you will have to put a lot at stake financially. This is a good thing because if you really want to do something, you'll figure out a way to make it happen, even if it isn't currently within your means to make the financial commitment.

On the flip side, I've experienced many times where once I commit to a goal, all types of opportunities open up that enable me to reach that goal. Therefore, be wary of making financial commitments that make you feel uncomfortable, but at the same time, also understand the source of the discomfort. If it isn't about the money then maybe it's the wrong goal to be pursuing at this time. My motto is that if something happens easily, it's meant to be. If something doesn't feel right to you at any time—wait.

Exercise 4.6: Balancing multiple requirements—using a decision matrix

In the previous activity, you may have felt uncomfortable about the financial commitment you identified that you would have to make to reach your goal. One of the reasons for this is that you may be uncertain about the impact that this one goal will have on your other life priorities and requirements. As mentioned in the personal experience section about my child's school, we were very uncomfortable about the school situation, yet we weren't ready to make a financial commitment to change the situation because we weren't sure how to balance it with the requirements of the rest of our small family. To get a handle on the best course of action for us, we developed a decision matrix. First we identified all our requirements together. Then we brainstormed all our options. Next we each ranked the requirements from least important to most important. Then we ranked each option—for its likelihood to help us meet each requirement. From this analysis, we were able to quantify our choices and balance our requirements. We were much more comfortable making a financial commitment once we were clear on the best course of action that would balance our multiple priorities.

In this exercise, you're going to go through this type of analysis step by step.

Why perform this exercise?

Often, when you are faced with having to balance a number of different requirements, it's easy to get overwhelmed and do nothing—thereby maintaining your same, stuck, status quo. This exercise will help you gather input from the other people affected by your decisions so you can develop a rational assessment of the best course of action.

Step 1: Identify your goal.

Example: Create a school/living situation for the kids where they will thrive.

Step 2: Identify the requirements needed to reach that goal. Have everyone who is participating in the decision making participate in identifying the requirements.

Example: Goal requirements for creating a school/living situation for the kids where they will thrive.

1. Good school—diverse, well-run science and math program, gifted program, music program, no lotteries

2. Mom's business can do well without Mom having to travel much

3. Live around friendly, happy, active, adventurous, outgoing people

4. See Dad more often

5. House we live in has at least three bedrooms and three bathrooms

6. See the grandparents at least once a month

7. Has both long- and short-term stability

Step 3: Each person ranks the requirements—a ranking of 5 denotes a "must have" while a ranking of 1 is "not important." Sum up the total for each requirement. List the requirements in column one of a spread sheet. Each person gets their own column and ranks the requirements. Create a total column that is the sum of each person's ranking for each requirement.

Step 4: Identify all your options to achieve your goal.

Example: Various options possible to create a school/living situation for the kids where they will thrive.

1. Stay in our current house in the current school.

2. Go to private school near our current house.

3. Move to another town with better schools.

4. Go live with Dad where the schools are better.

Step 5: For each option, identify how well it helps meet the requirements—a ranking of 5 denotes a "most likely" while a ranking of -5 is "least likely." Create a column for each option and put in the ranking for how well that option meets the requirements.

Step 6: Do the math. Multiply the total requirement ranking by the option ranking for each option and each requirement. Sum the numbers for each option.

Example: For our assessment, the top option immediately became apparent and I was able to make a financial commitment to pursue our goal. We decided to stay where we were and find a suitable private school. Overall, this option best met our requirements.

Wrap up

Assessing your finances can be like getting a cold bucket of water tossed in your face. However, this step is crucial if you want to consciously create your existence in this material plane. Having bills to pay constructs the work-day reality for the majority of people on the planet. You can choose how those bills will affect your day-to-day life.

Reflections

Take a few minutes to reflect on what you learned doing these exercises:

1. What did you learn by first looking at your net worth and then understanding how your financial commitments have created your reality?

2. How did you feel doing these exercises? Why do you think you felt that way?

3. What changes are you going to make in your life because of what you learned doing these exercises?

"Many people fail in life, not for lack of ability or brains or even courage but simply because they have never organized their energies around a goal."

Elbert Hubbard

Chapter 5

Spiritual Truth #5: Money Needs to Flow

Visualize yourself as a pond. Money flows into your pond in the form of earned income and "unearned income" from investments, gifts, etc. It also flows out of your pond in the form of utility bills, phone bills, grocery bills, and insurance bills. And it flows into other ponds—into retirement accounts, college savings funds, and investment accounts.

When the money comes into your pond, what happens if you just leave it there? Like any pond, if the water isn't flowing, it will stagnate. If the water is clean or water is in short supply and other people need it, they'll figure out a way to get

> *"Money needs to flow for it to have value."*

it and thereby start it flowing again. Money needs to flow for it to have "value." When I viewed the flow of money with me as the pond, it became clear to me that the way the money flowed out of my pond influenced the nature and amount of money that flowed into my pond. I also realized that the money flowing out of my pond could enable other systems to exist.

When I first visualized the pond metaphor to money, I literally had four different attorneys working on different legal issues. I had a family-law attorney fighting off my ex-husband who was trying to get me to pay for all of his visits to see our children while trying to gain custody of them at the same time. I had a corporate attorney fighting a former business partner who wanted 40% of the company profits for doing 0% of the work. I had a labor attorney evaluating a lawsuit on my behalf against a former employer for breach of contract. And I had an intellectual-property attorney representing my interests with intellectual property I had negotiated ownership of with that same former employer.

I was beside myself because all of these attorneys were draining a huge sum of money from my pond, and because I didn't want to live my life this way. It dawned on me that a system only exists when you continue to put energy into it. I didn't want some of these systems to exist in my life so I stopped putting money into them.

I fired the family-law attorney—I represented myself and outlasted my ex-husband with his cases. His attorney ate up all of his resources so he couldn't continue to pursue me. I decided to just ignore the business partner—he went away. I decided not to pursue the breach of contract against the former employer, and I put the intellectual-property attorney on the back burner until I really needed their help with filing patents, trade-marks, and devising a risk management strategy for the company. I stopped putting money (and energy) into systems that I didn't want to exist, and they ceased to exist and ceased being a problem in my life.

Next I started to analyze how the money coming out of my pond was influencing the money coming into my pond. I soon realized that to increase the money coming into my pond, I needed to focus on how the money coming out could dramatically increase the money coming into the pond. So I tightened up the direct correlations between money out and money in.

For example, for every dollar I spent on advertising, I wanted to see at least $10 coming into the pond. For every new employee I hired, I wanted to see at least a four-fold increase in money coming into the pond. With the new money coming into the pond, it's given me an opportunity to expand into new areas and grow the company. Instead of "me" being the pond, I now have a whole company and the pond is getting bigger to handle a larger in-flow and out-flow of money.

In this chapter, you are going to analyze your own pond. First you're going to identify the money flowing into your pond. Next you're going to identify the money flowing out of your pond. Then you're going to look at how the money coming out of your pond enables the money to flow into your pond. In the last exercise, you're going to become a money-flow engineer and figure out how to make the money flowing out of your pond increase the flow rate of money back into your pond.

Exercise 5.1: Map your pond. In this exercise, you draw a picture of your cash-flow pond—the money that comes in, the size and characteristics of the pond based on how you feel about it, and the money that goes out.

Exercise 5.2: Your existing system. In this exercise, you identify how your overall cash-flow system works so you have a starting point for redesigning a system that may better suit your needs.

Exercise 5.3: Your redesigned system. In this exercise, you draw a pond the way you'd like it to be.

Exercise 5.4: Your five-year plan. In this exercise, you identify your year-to-year goals to create your redesigned cash flow system.

Exercise 5.1: Map your pond

Identify all the sources of money that flow into your pond. The more money flowing from a single source, the wider and longer the arrow should be (just as you would depict the size of pond-feeding rivers and streams). Draw what your pond feels like to you—is it small, or large? Is it bordered with reeds, stagnated by excessive growth, or is it a clean, deep, clear-running pond bordered by stark sheer cliffs on either side—relatively inaccessible? Identify all the money that flows out of your pond. The more money that flows out to any one source, the wider and longer the arrow should be. You can even annotate dollar amounts on these arrows if you want.

Why perform this exercise?

Illustrating your financial reality with a picture that indicates cash flow in and out of your "pond" may help you move beyond an abstract concept of money to a new, more productive way of looking at it and your net worth.

Exercise 5.2: The existing "system"

Imagine that the money flowing out of your pond actually creates the siphon for the money flowing back into your pond. If the flow of money out of your pond is blocked, as true for water, the money will be diverted to other ponds or cause other calamitous effects such as floods. To keep money flowing, you need to understand the dynamics of your cash flow situation. The way you use the money in your pond in fact creates the money coming into your pond. For this exercise, identify how the money going out of your pond helps you create the sources of money coming into your pond.

Why perform this exercise?

When you start to understand your own cash flow "system" then you can start to engineer a system that is more aligned with your overall goals and ambitions.

Exercise 5.3: The redesigned "system"

This is your chance to dream. Now that you're used to thinking in terms of money flowing, draw a picture of the type of pond you want to create. Record all the feelings that you have about your new pond and money flowing system. Identify how you feel about the money coming in, how you feel about the size and characteristics of your pond and how you feel about the money going out.

Why perform this exercise?

The first step toward creating what you want is to be able to visualize what you want. When you attach feelings to what you want to create, then it becomes even more real. Often we get so caught up in the minutiae of day-to-day life that we forget about our goals, aspirations and dreams. If you can make a powerful picture of your dreams and attach feelings to it, you'll better remember it. If you can better remember it, you have a better chance of staying the course to actualize your dreams.

Exercise 5.4: Your five-year plan

Assess how your cash flow might change over the next five years. Identify how your sources of money flowing in may change and how the requirements for money flowing out might change. For each change, assess the probability of that change occurring, the impact it will have on your "pond" and your ability to affect the change. For changes that have the highest probability of happening and have the greatest impact (either good or bad) evaluate the level of planning you need to do now to manage those changes.

Why perform this exercise?

Sometimes we worry needlessly about changes that have a very low probability of occurring. This exercise helps you develop the wisdom to accept the things you cannot change, the courage to change the things you can change, and the intelligence to know the difference.

Wrap up

Hoarding hard-earned cash, or conversely, not being conscious of how your money slips through your fingers and out through all the creases and crevices of your life puts money in charge of you instead of making you in charge of your life. You can create the situation where money flows in the direction that will create the most long-term value for you. You can establish a money-flow system in your life that works to help you achieve your goals.

Reflections

Take a few minutes to reflect on what you learned doing these activities:

1. What did you learn by looking at your "pond" of money and how it flows in and out of your life?

2. How did you feel doing these exercises? Why do you think you felt that way?

3. What changes are you going to make in your life because of what you learned doing these exercises?

"Make your life a mission—not an intermission."

Arnold H. Glasglow

Chapter 6
Spiritual Truth #6: Paying It Forward Improves Cash Flow

Like most Americans my age, I was raised to believe that I needed a credit card for "emergencies." Yes, maybe 20 years ago that was true. It is no longer true with the ready access to cash, your cash, through the ATM machines and debit cards that act just like credit cards. As you age and pay your bills on time, credit card companies give you more and more credit. Credit can start to give you a false sense of prosperity—especially in times when money isn't flowing into your "pond" that well, but you still have the same outflow requirements (i.e. like when you lose a job).

In my early 30s I had the ability to access over $50,000 in unsecured money—that is, money I could take and use any way I wanted to use it. It wasn't secured by a house as collateral as is a mortgage. It was money I could use and pay back at my "leisure." What I didn't realize at the time was that having this much money at my disposal literally blocked the flow of money to me from other sources. This was not my money, it was the banks' money that I could use now with the expectation that I'd have to pay it back later.

I'm an entrepreneur and an entrepreneur makes it or breaks it based on creatively bringing ideas to market. I've found time and time again that the most creative and successful ideas are developed when you're backed up against the wall and have to come up with a solution so you can pay your bills. If you have credit cards, they give you an easy way out and those creative inspirations just won't happen. If you don't have access to credit cards or easy unsecured debt, YOU can come up with many ideas to make money and the universe does seem to provide. I've experienced this time and time again: When I have "easy" money at my disposal, the universe has already provided. I don't get the ideas as quickly or as effectively out to market.

At one time, we experienced this truth on a very big level. One of the key players in the company was continually counseling me to get a line of credit to cover payroll in the event of an emergency. We had the "emergency." We rolled out a new registration system for our courses and the company that was doing our registrations was not in a position to pay us over $110,000 in revenues they collected on our behalf since they were using our money to cover their operational expenses. We had to meet a $50,000 per month payroll. Luckily our new registration system was working well and money was flowing into our company faster. However, we still had the cash shortfall.

> *"The most creative and successful ideas are developed when you're backed up against the wall"*

We had a meeting with the top line of the company and creatively brainstormed ways to generate more sales to be able to cover payroll. And guess what, our sales doubled— putting us even further ahead. If we had the line of credit to bail us out—we would not have been as motivated to take some of the aggressive measures we did with marketing and sales.

Necessity is truly the mother of invention. With easy access to credit, you eliminate the necessity that inspires the very inventions that will enable you to be successful.

Not only can the easy access to credit stifle innovation but the "pay back later" concept can completely dry up your pond. You spend your life "servicing your debt" rather than putting money into systems that you want to build up. If you find yourself with an excessive amount of unsecured credit (or debt), and money is not flowing into your life the way you'd like it to, GET RID OF ALL OF YOUR CREDIT CARDS. You do not need them, and they block your flow of money. Move to a pay-by-cash system for all of your day-to-day and travel purchases.

The only thing you should ever consider financing is an appreciating asset—one that increases in value at least equal to, if not greater than the cost of the money to finance that asset. For example, if you get a mortgage on a house, and the interest rate is 7% per year, make sure the homes in the area are appreciating at least 7% per year in value. This way, you have money flowing into your pond (the increasing value of your house) at least equal to the money flowing out of your pond (your mortgage payment).

I've heard all the arguments for keeping the credit cards—I need them for "emergencies," I need them because I earn frequent flyer mileage, I pay off the balances every month. First of all, you don't need them for emergencies. There are six billion people on this planet—any "emergency" that you find yourself in, there are literally thousands of people who can help you get out of it. At the lowest of low points in my life financially, my car broke down on the way to visit my brother. My sister helped me out with her AAA gold card and we had the car towed 100 miles back to my town. My partner showed up with his car and loaned it to me for a week (he felt great about doing this—people like to help people). A couple picked us up off the highway and drove us to a nearby gas station. NOTHING BAD HAPPENED— and we had some fun because of the whole experience. If I had the credit cards, I would've had the car towed to a local garage and gotten a rental car. The whole ordeal would've likely had cost me $1,000 more than it cost me.

If you need emergency cash, figure out how much you need and get it into an interest bearing account so that way your emergency nest egg is making you money. Second, you can get a debit card with very high-per-day daily limits to cover what you would normally use a credit card to purchase. This debit card will also give you mileage on your frequent flyer program. I travel extensively, and $5,000 per day covers most of what I get into with travel. If you really need more than a $5,000-per-day daily limit—have several accounts with several debit cards

Even if you pay off the balances on your credit cards every month, you are time delaying the flow of YOUR money. When you purchase something using a credit card, you are not using your money. This is not a money flow into your pond. The money is only flowing out of your pond to the credit card company. Yes, you have "acquired" goods or services with money from the credit card, but it was not your money and by the time you get around to paying for that item, what you purchased already decreased or ceased to have any value—thereby not having a flow or "value" of money into your pond.

For example, let's say you go out to dinner, and you pay $50 for that meal. You put it on your credit card. The credit card company just paid for that dinner. By the time you get around to paying the credit card company for the meal, the meal has long ago ceased to be of value to you. New money flowing into your system has to be diverted to pay for something you already bought—you're essentially making your money swim upstream. Credit cards disrupt the natural flow of money into and out of your life. Now imagine that you use a debit card for the same meal. Once you've paid for the meal, you're done. You don't have to use the new money flowing into your life from that point forward to pay for that meal you just had. If you want more money flowing into your life, faster, you need to stop having your money swim upstream. Get rid of the time-delay factor you're incurring.

If you're already in over your head with credit cards—get rid of all your cards IMMEDIATELY. Even if you aren't yet in over your head, GET RID OF ALL YOUR CARDS IMMEDIATELY. You don't need them. There are numerous agencies and attorneys who can negotiate on your behalf with credit card companies to get your payments reduced, the amount you owe reduced, and who can help you get out of the credit card quagmire.

For every credit card I got rid of, I doubled the flow of money into my pond. First I got rid of the heavy hitters, the ones with the $15,000 line of credit, and then I moved my way down. I got rid of the last credit card, a stupid little department store credit card that was still in my married name. I owed less than $300 on it. Once that last card was gone, my income literally doubled every month. If you haven't caught on yet—GET RID OF YOUR CREDIT CARDS—and watch what starts to happen to the money flowing into your life.

These exercises are crucial for getting more money flowing into your life. There are two fundamental ones here:

Exercise 6.1: Unsecured debt. In this exercise you evaluate all the places in your life where you have grown dependent on unsecured debt.

Exercise 6.2: Curing unsecured debt addictions. In this exercise you create a plan to free yourself of the need to rely on unsecured debt to achieve your goals.

Exercise 6.1: Unsecured debt

Take stock of all the unsecured debt you have: Credit card bills for services already rendered, student loans, others. List all the debt. Figure out a payment schedule or contact a consumer credit counseling agency or Lexington Legal Law clinic to help you out of them (I do not recommend you roll your unsecured debt into a "home equity" loan—you're basically taking a low risk debt and turning it into a high risk debt).

Why perform this exercise?

Many people are in complete denial about the amount of unsecured debt in their life. Yes they know it is there and it literally sucks their life force from them. Get real about what you owe so that you can start to create a plan to be free of this way of life.

Exercise 6.2: Curing unsecured debt addictions

QUIT COLD TURKEY. JUST DO IT. Set up an account specifically for making debit card purchases. Debit cards that are attached to your main accounts are risky because if you lose your card, the person who gets your card can drain all the money from your account. At the time this book was written, Chase Manhattan bank offered a debit card with a $5000 daily limit. Get on the Internet and find banks that offer debit cards with high daily limits. Get one of these cards and put as much money in there as you think you will need for your standard credit card purchases or your "emergencies." Just stop using your credit cards and work with a team of professionals to 'discharge" your credit card debt. You do not need to file bankruptcy to do this or ruin your credit report. You just need the will to do it.

Why perform this exercise?

It will open up the flood gates of money to you once you take back your life force from the life sucking problems that credit card debt causes. Even if you don't have credit card debt and pay off your balance every month, you are still causing your money to flow backwards and you have a false sense of prosperity.

Wrap up

This is a very easy concept to talk about but quite another to actually implement. We live in a materialistic, instant gratification society. Once you get rid of your credit cards you will see that the universe really does provide for you. Take the leap.

Reflections

Spend a few minutes reflecting on what you experienced doing these exercises:

1. What did you learn by analyzing your debt and about the prospect of giving up your credit cards? What is the worse thing that could happen to you?

2. How did you feel when you looked at your debt and considered giving up your credit cards?

3. How are you going to use this information to improve the quality of your life?

"Man is a goal seeking animal.
His life only has meaning if he is reaching out
and striving for his goals."

Aristotle

Chapter 7
Spiritual Truth #7: Wealth Is a State of Mind

Wealth is a state of abundance; poverty is a state of scarcity. We live in an infinitely abundant world. Your desires create your state of mind. If you're constantly in a state of "want"—while at the same time believe that you can't get what you want then you will forever live in a state of poverty. If you're satisfied with what you have, and know that you can get whatever it is you want, you will forever live in a state of wealth. Wealth has nothing to do with the balance in your bank account, unless that is what it is you want—a big bank account. There are people who feel wealthy who have no income at all and there are "impoverished" millionaires.

The next couple of exercises help you develop your wealthy state of mind.

Exercise 7.1: The wealth dream

If you had all the money you ever needed, what would you be doing right now?

- How would you feel?

- How would your life be different than it is right now?

- What would you need to give up in order to create this type of life for yourself?

- What would need to happen for you to achieve this? (You can say win the lottery if you want to, but you'll also need to come up with some other strategies as well because the probability of winning the lottery is pretty slim. You need to have another plan in place in case winning the lottery doesn't pan out.)

My personal journey

If I had all the money I ever needed what would I be doing right now? I'd be feeling very comfortable and content—I term this the full-belly bank account. My life is essentially in this state right now. I was fretting that my retirement account was not as large as it should be, until watching the tanking of the stock market. Now I'm quite happy with how I've managed things. I would be starting to purchase more real estate since that is where I earn more money anyhow, but I realize that comes with a price of having people maintain that real estate. I'm learning how to do that. To create this type of life for myself I need to give up some "control" and allow the people who want to help me to help me. To achieve this, I need to become clear about the type of life and existence I'd like to create for myself and look long term at the ramifications of my decisions.

When I looked at this further, I realized that wealth to me is about comfort. I live my life to create new experiences for myself, and some of the "experiences" I find myself in where I'm "uncomfortable" have far more to do with a lack of preparedness for that experience than lack of money to explore the different realms of that experience. For example, I travel extensively. I once dreamed that it would be fun to teleport—that is, with the blink of an eye (like the genie in I Dream of Genie used to do) I'd be where I wanted to go. Then I started to realize that the journey was part of the fun of travel. I prefer to take the more public forms of transportation when I'm traveling because I meet more people. If I had my own jet, I wouldn't meet as many people. I live my life alone for the most part, so traveling gives me the opportunity to meet new people. ◆

Exercise 7.2: How would "wealth" change your life, right now?

If you were "wealthy" how would you be living your life differently than you do now?

> ## My personal journey
>
> Wealth means to me making money without the efforts of my direct labor—where money just flows into my accounts because of the money making systems I put in place. Right now I'm struggling with the idea of developing new adventure-based courses in Alaska. This nagging voice in the back of my head says—is that real-estate purchase going to generate passive income? I don't know a thing about renting property—but I do know how to make money by running training courses. My brother is into real estate and judges real-estate acquisitions strictly by how much money he can make from the rent, so he typically judges the decisions by which I make real-estate transactions by a different benchmark than I do. Wealth means to me that I have my business models fully developed so that when I make my real-estate transactions to support the business concepts I have, they work to meet my end objectives. I don't concern myself with anyone else's measurement of my success but my own. ◆

Exercise 7.3: Wealth perspectives

We are far wealthier now just from a creature comfort perspective than we have ever been in the past. Analyze your day-to-day life and identify ways that you are wealthier than people from 100 years ago:

- The type of dwelling you live in? Is it easier to upkeep? More than likely, with the advances in building technology.

- Access to food? Do you spend less time in the acquisition and preparation of your meals than people did 100 years ago? Most likely, with the modern supermarket and convenience factors.

- Method by which you get to work or to pick up the materials you need to live day to day? We are far more mobile today than we were 100 years ago, and many of us even have the luxury of working from wherever we want because of telecommunications and computer technologies.

- What you do for vacation and recreation? We have the means to travel far more extensively and at a far lower cost than all previous generations.

My personal journey

I live in a modest house in a modest neighborhood. The "weather inside" my house is a stable 68 to 72 degrees. I have beautifully clean, running water to drink and to bathe in, and I have a wonderful yard with a nice garden. My home is by no means in a "wealthy" neighborhood—but I consider myself extremely wealthy because of all the creature comforts it provides. I spend less than one hour per day in acquiring food or preparing meals. and considering that I don't have any servants helping me out, that is amazing. I do go berry-picking several times a year, but that is for fun. As far as picking up what I need to live day to day—I can order just about anything I want from the Internet, and it will be delivered to my door. I also have a very reliable car that I can easily get serviced whenever I need. I travel at the drop of a hat to places around the world very inexpensively. Compared to even my parents' existence at my age, I live a much more prosperous and abundant lifestyle. ◆

Wrap up

You can be wealthy with pennies to your name and a pauper with millions in the bank. Your perceptions of wealth have absolutely nothing to do with your bank balance and everything to do with your perspective. To become truly wealthy, work on your perspective.

Reflections

Take a couple minutes to evaluate what you learned and experienced doing these activities in this chapter and in this book:

1. What are the top three things that you learned doing the activities in this book? How will you recall this information next month, next year?

2. How did you feel doing the activities in this book? What changed about your perceptions as you went through the activities?

3. What are you going to do with what you learned from the activities? How can you best sustain the changes you want to make?

Conclusion

You can achieve your goals and dreams. For most, these Seven Spiritual Truths are just reminders of what you already know. If you'd like to learn more, visit www.spiritualmoney. com where you can register to take our Project Prosperity course.

"Many persons have the wrong idea of what constitutes true happiness. It is not attained through self-gratification but through fidelity to a worthy purpose."

Helen Keller

About Cheetah Learning

Headquartered in Carson City, NV, with licensed training providers worldwide, Cheetah Learning is a global leader in Project Management professional development and a market leader in Accelerated Learning. Cheetah was founded in 1999 with the firm belief that people can reach their goals quickly with the right tools and training. Cheetah Learning created the patent-pending Accelerated Exam Prep™ methodology that is the basis of its highly successful Cheetah Exam Prep® for the PMP® Course.

Tens of thousands of project managers worldwide have gone through the Cheetah program. From negotiations to Project Management leadership, Cheetah's accelerated learning techniques enable people to become more effective, FAST. Many of Cheetah's courses are authorized to receive college credits. A PMI Registered Education Provider and an authorized IACET training provider, Cheetah delivers courses at training centers worldwide, at client locations and online at www.cheetahpm.com

Suggested Reading

Canfield, Jack L., Mark Victor Hansen and Les Hewitt. 2000. *Power of Focus: How to Hit Your Business, Personal and Financial Targets with Absolute Certainty*. Deerfield Beach, FL: Health Communications, Inc.

Carnegie, Dale, Arthur R. Pell (Editor) and Dorothy Carnegie (Editor). 1990. *How to Win Friends and Influence People*. New York: Simon & Schuster.

Csikszentmihalyi, Mihaly. 1991. *Flow: The Psychology of Optimal Experience*.

New York: Harper Collins.

Gerber, Michael E. 1998. *The E-Myth: Do You Have a Business or a Job?*

Gitomer, Jeffrey. 1998. *Customer Satisfaction Is Worthless, Customer Loyalty Is Priceless: How to Make Customers Love You, Keep Them Coming Back and Tell Everyone They Know*. New York: Bard Press.

Gladwell, Malcolm. 2002. *The Tipping Point: How Little Things Can Make a Big Difference*. London: Little Brown & Company.

Glasser, William. 1999. *Choice Theory: A New Psychology of Personal Freedom*. New York: HarperCollins Publishers.

Kiyosaki, Robert T. and Sharon L. Lechter. 2000. *Rich Dad, Poor Dad: What the Rich Teach Their Kids About Money—That the Poor and Middle Class Do Not!* New York: Warner Business Books.

Kiyosaki, Robert T. with Sharon L. Lechter. 2003. *Rich Dad's Success Stories: Real Life Success Stories from Real Life People Who Followed the Rich Dad Lessons.* New York: Warner Business Books.